LIFE'S LESSONS FROM MY CAT

BY TONI GOFFE

First published in Great Britain by
Pendulum Gallery Press
56 Ackender Road, Alton, Hants GU34 1JS

© TONI GOFFE 1994

LIFE'S LESSONS FROM MY CAT
ISBN 0-948912-27-8

PRINTED IN GREAT BRITAIN BY
UNWIN BROTHERS LTD, OLD WOKING, SURREY

NLY LIVE WITH A FAMILY
HAT CAN FULLY SUPPORT
OU.

ONE DAY EAT LIVER -------
THE NEXT DAY REFUSE IT.
THIS MAKES YOU LOOK
LIKE AN EXPERT.

NEVER EAT FOOD FROM ---
A TIN.

SLEEP ALL DAY BECAUSE--
YOU`LL BE OUT ALL NIGHT
HAVING

FUN!

YOU`VE GOT **NINE** LIVES
GO FOR IT.

PEOPLE LOVE THEIR
STOMACHS----------------
--------PUMMLED.

LEARN TO PURRRRRRRR

FISH IS GOOD FOR-------
THE BRAIN.

LEARN TO JUGGLE.

BE
SUPERIOR,
YOU
KNOW
YOU
ARE

DO CUTE THINGS

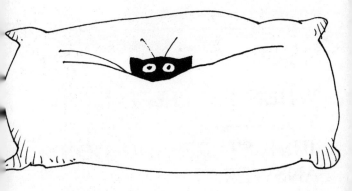

WHEN PEOPLE TALK TO
YOU--------
JUST STARE AND DON`T
ANSWER.

GET TO KNOW
SOMEONE--------------------
WITH A TROUT FARM.

DON`T FEEL GUILTY.

IF IN DOUBT ------------
WASH YOURSELF.

DON'T WATCH T.V.

DON`T LET
 ANYONE
ELSE WATCH IT
EITHER.

STARING AT THE MOON
MAKES YOU LOOK---------
INTELLIGENT.

FIND YOUR PLACE
IN THE **SUN**.

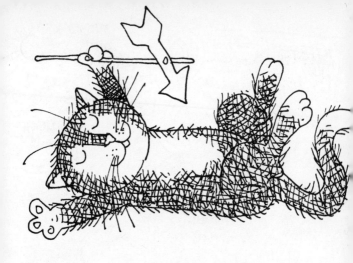

WHEN YOU`RE STRESSED
OUT ----------------
GET SOMEONE TO
STROKE YOUR TUMMY.

NINE----------
IS YOUR LUCKY NUMBER.

BEWARE OF ANYONE WHO
LOOKS LIKE A DOG.............

HAVE NO CONCERNS OVER
MONEY.

SLEEP IN INTERESTING
PLACES.

DON`T BE AFRAID TO
EXPERIMENT----

WHEN YOU`RE LONELY,
LIE FACE DOWN TILL
SOMEONE COMES BY AND
TURNS YOU OVER----------

WHEN SOMEONE IS
TALKING TO YOU----------
SHUT YOUR EYES---------
IT DRIVES PEOPLE
CRAZY.

PEOPLE LOVE YOU
SITTING ON THEIR LAPS
-------------EVEN STRANGERS.

NEVER SLEEP ALONE
----------------ALWAYS ON A
HUMAN.

TWO TYPES OF MUSIC---
NOT TO LIKE -------------------
COUNTRY & WESTERN.
(TOO MANY FIDDLES).

DRINKING WATER IS
HEALTHY--------------------
BUT CREAM IS NICER.

ALWAYS SEND BACK THE
------------ FIRST COURSE.

ALWAYS BE FUSSY WITH
--------------YOU`RE FOOD.

ALWAYS LEAVE A LITTLE
FOOD ON YOUR PLATE----
FOR LATER.

RATS MAKE A GREAT
----------------SUPRISE GIFT.

BEWARE OF CATS
CALLED TOM.

NEVER EAT ------------
 OUT OF SOMEONE ELSE`S
FOOD DISH.

GET TO KNOW SOME
----------FAT CATS.

ONLY LIVE IN TOWNS
------------ THE COUNTRY`S
GOING TO THE DOGS.

BE PLAYFUL ---------
   LIGHTEN UP--------
      HAVE SOME FUN

WHEN SOMEONE OFFERS
YOU A DRINK ------------------
TAKE ONE.
BUT DON`T GIVE
ANYTHING IN RETURN.......

SLEEP WHERE EVER
YOU WANT TO.

IF YOU`RE PICKED UP
-------------------RELAX..

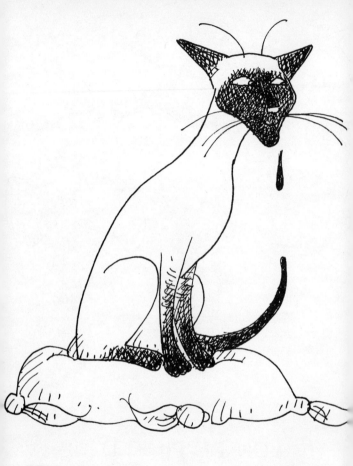

IF YOU`RE NOT GETTING
ENOUGH ATTENTION--------
---------- BITE SOMEBODY.

SNIFF EVERYTHING --------
-----YOU`RE GIVEN.

BE DIFFERENT.

SLEEP AROUND.

" IT`S
 RAINING
CATS & DOGS"-----
IS ONLY HEARSAY.

BE CURIOUS -----------
BUT BE CAREFUL.

CURIOSITY--------
NEVER KILLED ANYONE
---------- BELIEVE ME.

ONLY KILL WHEN YOU
------------ HAVE TO.

KILLING TIME NEVER
HURT ANYONE.

ALWAYS COVER UP YOUR
----------------WRONG DOINGS.

IF THEY WONT LET YOU
IN-----------------
SIT ON THEIR WINDOW
SILL TILL THEY DO.

SIT BY A DOOR-----------
SOMEONE INTERESTING
MIGHT OPEN IT FOR YOU.

NEVER SWIM IN WATER,
----IT MAKES PUSSY WET.

DON`T HAVE ANYTHING
TO DO WITH RAIN, DOGS,
AND VIOLINS.

BE A COOOOOOL CAT.

IT`S NOT OLD FASHIONED
TO BE A HEP-CAT.

BE STREET - WISE.

CATS ARE WHERE ITS AT.

OTHER BOOKS IN THIS
SERIES; BY TONI GOFFE

IS THERE LIFE WITHOUT
CATS ?   ISBN 0.948912.21.9

IS THERE LIFE WITHOUT
DOGS ?   ISBN 0.948912.22.7

LIFE`S LESSONS FROM
MY DOG. ISBN 0.948912.28.6

LOVE CATS ISBN 0.948912.30.8